私たちは座ろ。

We
Sit

We Sit

Paintings *by* MARLEY KAUL

Poems by TAIJU GERI WILIMEK

Published by Mill Studio Press
4111 Mill Street NE
Bemidji, MN 56601
www.marleykaul.com
millstudiopress@midco.net

Published in the United States of America

Printed on acid-free, archival-quality paper by CG Book Printers, Mankato, Minnesota

Edited by KathleenWeflen
Cover and interior design by Lynn Phelps

ISBN: 978-1-7323894-0-3

1. Art. 2. Poetry. 3. Egg Tempera. 4. Zen.
Library of Congress Control Number: 2018907314

FIRST EDITION

Kaul, Marley, 1939–
Wilimek, Taiju Geri, 1953–
We Sit/Paintings by Marley Kaul, Poems by Taiju Geri Wilimek

For *Julia Marie DeLeone*, my youngest grandchild, whose humor, love, and understanding have carried me away from gloom to laughter and blue skies.

—*Marley Kaul*

For *Jay*, the only one who could be my husband, the most naturally compassionate and loyal person I know.

—*Geri Wilimek*

INTRODUCTION

In this book we—painter and poet—offer the fruits of contemplative practice. Each of us has been, for many years, interested in the dynamics of life and death, as they arise every day. The paintings presented here took shape through the slow process required by the centuries-old medium of egg tempera. The poems unfolded through zazen, the ancient practice of being still, alert, and observant of everyday life.

We both begin with present moment observations of ordinary experience, hone our attention, and find expression in painting and in writing poetry. For artist and writer alike, once a focus has been established in a given work, the "subject" takes on a

MATTHEW MCLAUGHLIN

life of its own. Without a precon-
ceived finish, each work develops
according to its own needs or
inclination, which can lead to a
surprising and sometimes enig-
matic resolution.

We share a respect for the
traditions of art and Zen. These
disciplines convey wisdom,
cultivate humanity, and enable us
to examine and express ourselves
and to connect with others.

The poems and paintings in
We Sit were made independently.
They are not intended as commen-
taries on one another, but we hope
you will find associations that are
intriguing and inspiring.

As you open the cover and enter
the space of this book, please join
us in our inquiry.

—*Marley Kaul* and *Taiju Geri Wilimek*

When I was a kid,

I remember my mom

cleaning house furiously

and midway through,

sitting down in the living room

on the cracked

naugahyde couch

with a cup of hot coffee

and a lit cigarette,

falling silent,

staring into

space.

This was my introduction

to meditation.

SECURE

The unspoken

is only regrettable

when it goes unnoticed

that the message

was not lost,

was fully received;

that flesh and bone

though mute, are enough;

more wise and articulate

than any poem

or dissertation.

Stepping outside

for a cool drink

of night air

soothing this

round hard ache

up under the sternum

somewhere close

to the heart.

I can't

find a name

for this draw

toward the company

of people who walk

on the edge,

where safety is desired

but not guaranteed,

where rapt attention is required

in order to navigate

with some semblance

of grace.

This poem is unfinished.

It seemed true when I wrote it.

One day it could ring false,

or it could become brighter

and smarter with time.

Then, it may just be

itself,

marking a moment.

Not the moment

it was written,

this one.

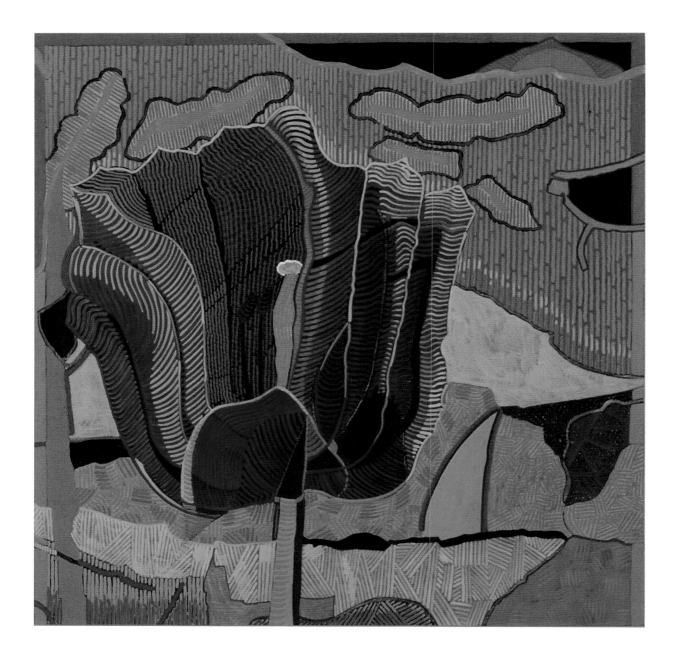

L o s s

Just wondering,

how are you going to do this?

The impossible has happened,

and everything

has turned into something

you don't want.

You are in life as it is,

and it isn't what you want.

The not-wanting penetrates

every cell and the spaces

in between every cell.

There is no undoing anything,

in fact, it's the other way around:

you are the thing undone.

How, how on earth

are you going to do this?

PRIMAL

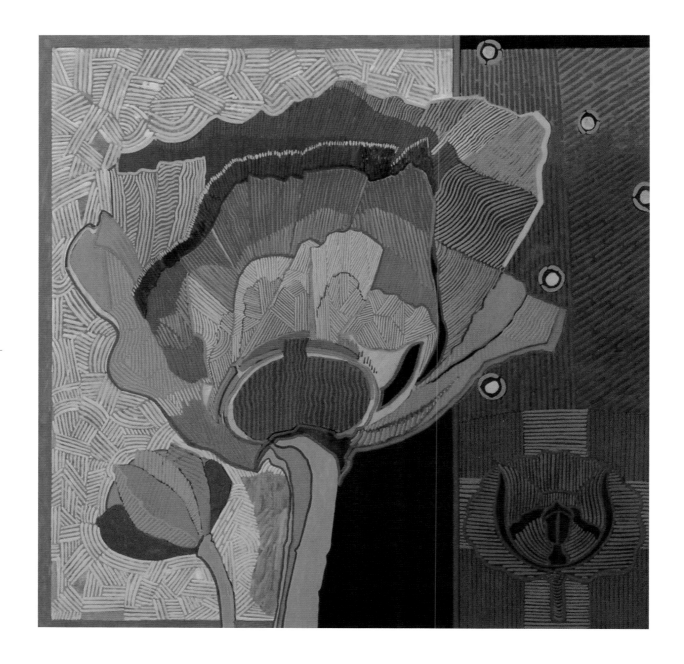

There are no statements,

only questions.

Do not be afraid of the pull
away from certainty.

So much is captured at high tide
and taken out to sea.

So much is left floundering,
struggling with gravity,
yearning for the return
of salt water and
sweet immersion.

ORIGIN

We sit

in clarity so brilliant it hurts.

This party is over.

A strange and difficult language

is forming as we gather anew.

Knowing, embedded since birth,

issues a message

so close to the bone

we must be still

in order to hear it.

And we really must sit together

in order to bear it.

TRUST

In this field

certain stones cannot be removed.

They hold their ground.

I plant and harvest around them.

They make for crooked rows;

take up productive space;

disintegrate only

a few molecules at a time.

I will be dissolved

into a billion particles of dust

before they budge.

WILL

Am I lazy,

sleeping

an hour past the alarm

then

heading straight

for the coffee pot,

then,

from this

spot on the couch

gazing out at

the morning

watching rabbits

eating the garden

and

squirrels gorging

at the bird feeder?

Grief arises here

in the laundry room,

facing a mountain of jumbled

sheets warm from the dryer.

Smelling a lifetime of

freshly made beds.

Faded color and wrinkles

that, stretched

across the mattress,

will surely smooth out.

Arms reaching wide and upward,

fingers squaring the corners,

folding, folding and folding again.

And there it is,

a compact flat oblong

that stacks neatly atop the others

on the closet shelf.

This morning is alive

with birdsong.

Cool air flows,

aspen leaves flutter,

a car passes on the road

unseen, but heard as an arc.

Shadows dance on the ground

and noticing them,

I see my aging foot:

dry, arthritic

with popping veins

and thick sole.

DESIRE

Day wanes
while
the full moon
brings me
close to bursting.

H E A L

One day

my mother

took up residence

in my body.

Face, skull

chest, belly and spine ...

all of it from sky to ground.

Now she inhabits me

in a friendly way,

going along with

almost

everything.

Asking why

will get you nowhere,

yet a question mark

is most honest, so

go ahead and

wonder!

She

is poised

over a large flowerpot

juicy red flowers

hanging from her mouth,

caught in the act,

gazing intently at me,

waiting to see whether

I bring arrogance or humility

to this situation.

Here is chicken soup.
Green zucchini, potatoes, carrots
and yellow egg noodles.

Here is a meal. Bowl, spoon
and eagerness.

Here is an empty pot
abandoned
on the stovetop.

Here is morning.
Scented soap, scratchy pad
and hot water.

Here are tiny shreds of white meat,
carrot fragments and potato skin

swirling down the drain,
never having dreamed
they'd end up
like this.

I am not this flower

that sways softly

its readiness to be seen,

yet what it has to do

with me is clear,

that I bring it into existence

with a glance,

and it completes everything

with utterly vivid red.

P E R S I S T E N T

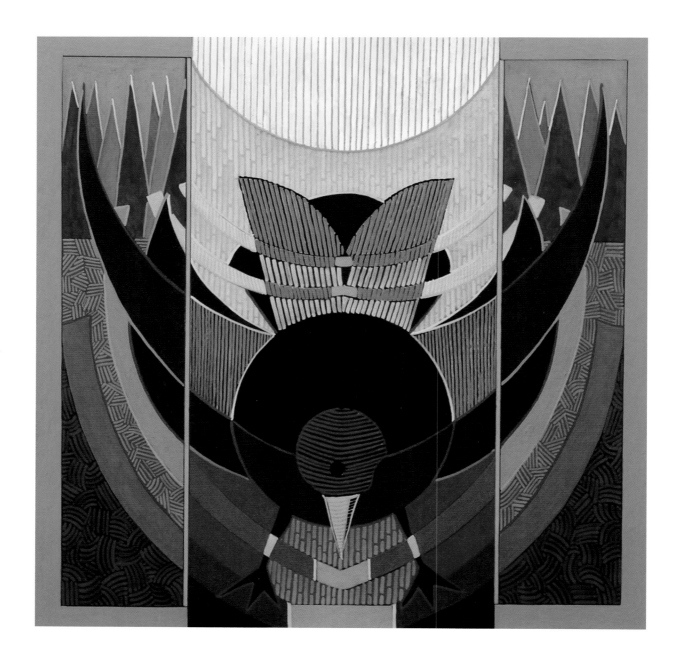

Know

this broken heart

in its full splendor.

Know this dark ache

as an echo in flesh,

from some broken part

that must be seen

with wide eyes

and in all honesty,

held.

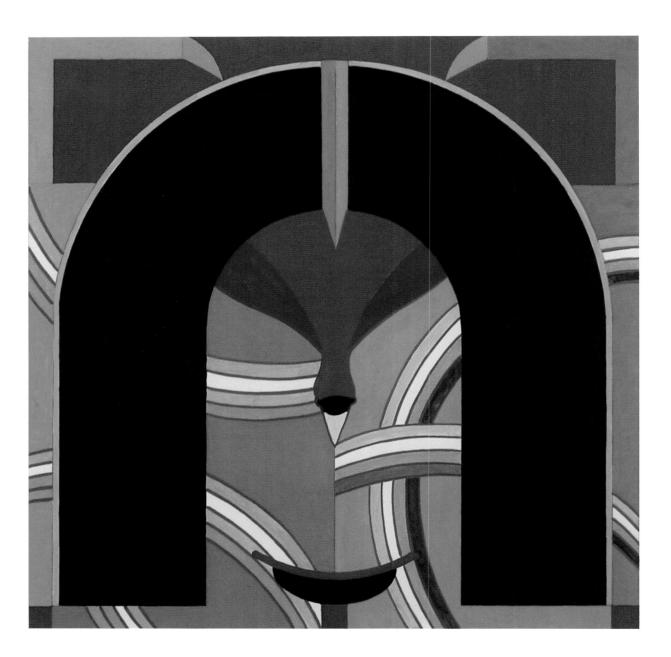

Upon arrival,
this monastery is
unbearably demanding.
There is no freedom,
only constant striving to
get things right.

There is stumbling
and bruising
as you try to please
the straight-faced,
silent master.

Sometimes
you beat on the gates,
hoping they will open.
They do not.

Sometimes
the gates swing open,
then close on your fingers
and you yelp.

Then one day you realize
a bird has flown in and made
a nest right on top
of your head.

Looking upward, you see:
the wide, smiling sky
was above you all along.

The locks fall to the ground,
the guards take their leave,
and the gates creak open,
then fall off their hinges.

The walls
east, west, north, and south
crumble.

And there you are:
giving and receiving
in the ten directions.

ABOUT THE PAINTER

Most of my life has been a search for authenticity. Who am I, where do I belong, and how will I achieve success?

I was born and raised on a farm in Good Thunder, Minnesota. My rural upbringing allowed for observation of all living things, gaining insights about death, birth, growth, and family beliefs. My search for authenticity continued through high school and university education, especially in sports and artistic endeavors. I became an artist, an educator, and a parent. I earned a Master of Fine Arts at the University of Oregon, and taught painting and drawing at Bemidji State University in northern Minnesota.

In the 1970s while in graduate school, I discovered meditation and Buddhist philosophy. Both have remained important to me and resurfaced in a new way recently when I received a medical diagnosis that forced me to confront my mortality. I allowed many visual constructs to influence my "new" method of working. Symbolism, symmetry, color, and size of work began to assert themselves. In less than a year, I completed the 20 egg tempera paintings included in this book. Each has a basic title, and each can serve as a prelude to meditation or prayer.

My paintings, acrylic and egg tempera, reside in private and public collections, including North Dakota Museum of Art, Plains Art Museum, Minnesota Historical Society, 3M Collections, Minnesota Mutual Life Collection, Tweed Museum of Art, Weisman Art Museum, and the Anderson Center. My memoir, *Letters to Isabella, Paintings by Marley Kaul,* was published in 2015.

I have been a professional painter for over 50 years. I paint daily in my studio near Lake Bemidji and exhibit throughout the northern region.

—*Marley Kaul*

ABOUT THE POET

I was born in 1950s coastal southern California, an environment of suburban order superimposed on a landscape of ocean, hilly grasslands, and snow-capped mountains, which you could see when not obscured by smog. I played in tide pools at the beach, never dreaming they were in jeopardy.

Poetry was introduced to me as a very young child by my grandmother, who read to me from her college English textbook. At the age of 8, I wrote my first poem, a rather haughty, judgmental rhyme about my little sister. My favorite book as a child was *Hailstones and Halibut Bones,* poetry about colors. I remember the thrill of discovering that poems need not rhyme, and could communicate rhythmically and graphically. During my teen years, I repeatedly read the works of e.e. cummings.

Although I completed degrees in Philosophy (BS) and Social Work (MSW), I have been most profoundly influenced by my everyday life. Becoming a mother, raising two daughters with my husband, and forming soulful friendships have all been essential. In my 40s, I had to face mortality with a diagnosis of breast cancer. Giving birth and facing death have been the most physically challenging and mind-clarifying experiences of my life. They have compelled me to fully occupy my life, vowing not to waste it.

The poems in this book are informed by more than a decade of practicing zazen, a Buddhist form of meditation that involves continual awareness of immediate experience. These poems come from moments of vivid awareness—first felt in the body—which I convert sparingly into written language. Poetry is a way of "putting myself out there" to find and communicate with other people; a gesture of caring for this life.

I am in private practice as a Licensed Independent Clinical Social Worker, and am an ordained monk in the Soto Zen tradition. Taiju is my given Buddhist name. I practice and teach meditation in both secular and Buddhist contexts.

My life and work today, including this book, arise out of all that has happened, and all that is possible.

—Taiju Geri Wilimek

Paintings

Egg tempera on panels, each 12 inches by 12 inches. *Slip* and *Secure*, 2016. All others, 2017.

———————————— ✥ ————————————

12 ~ *Slip*	28 ~ *Trust*	38 ~ *Heal*
14 ~ *Secure*	30 ~ *Will*	40 ~ *Place*
16 ~ *Drift*	32 ~ *Doubt*	42 ~ *Dance*
18 ~ *Guardian*	34 ~ *Tracks*	44 ~ *Descent*
20 ~ *Pause*	36 ~ *Desire*	46 ~ *Ritual*
22 ~ *Loss*		48 ~ *Persistent*
24 ~ *Primal*		50 ~ *We*
26 ~ *Origin*		

POEMS

COLOPHON

Typefaces
Batang, Microsoft, a Korean font with a mincho (serif) stroke style.
Copyright HanYang I&C Co., LTD. 2000

Cochin standard, Adobe Font Collection, first produced in 1912 by Georges Peignot at his foundry in Paris, named after 18th-century French engraver Charles-Nicolas Cochin.

Dalliance Flourishes, Emigre, designed by Frank Heine in 2000, based on elegant handwriting found on a map of a battle between the Habsburg Coalition and France at Ostrach, Germany, in 1799.

Soukou Mincho, Japanese font based on the open source font Source Han Serif, released by Flop Design. Strong contrast between vertical stems and horizontal arm strokes makes this a readable font with visual impact.

Cover and interior design
Lynn Phelps

Paper
Cover, matte lamination on 100-pound, acid-free Pacesetter gloss
Text, 100-pound, acid-free Pacesetter matte

Offset printing
CG Book Printers

Binding
CG Book Printers
Smyth-sewn perfect bound. Smyth sewing uses binder thread to stitch together a group of folded pages, known as a signature. Signatures are sewn together then bound with adhesive to the cover to create a book that opens wide and lays flat. Smyth-sewn binding has a reputation for being durable and long-lasting.

私たちは座ろ。